Earth: Measuring Its Changes

by Barbara M. Linde

Table of Contents

Pictures To Think About i
Words To Think About iii
Introduction 2
Chapter 1 Earthquakes 4
Chapter 2 Glaciers 13
Chapter 3 Water and Wind Erosion 22
Conclusion 29
Solve This Answers 30
Glossary 31
Index 32

Pictures To Think About

Juan de Fuca Plate

North American Plate

Caribbean Plate

Cocos Plate

Pacific Plate

Mazca Plate

South American Plate

i

Earth: Measuring Its Changes

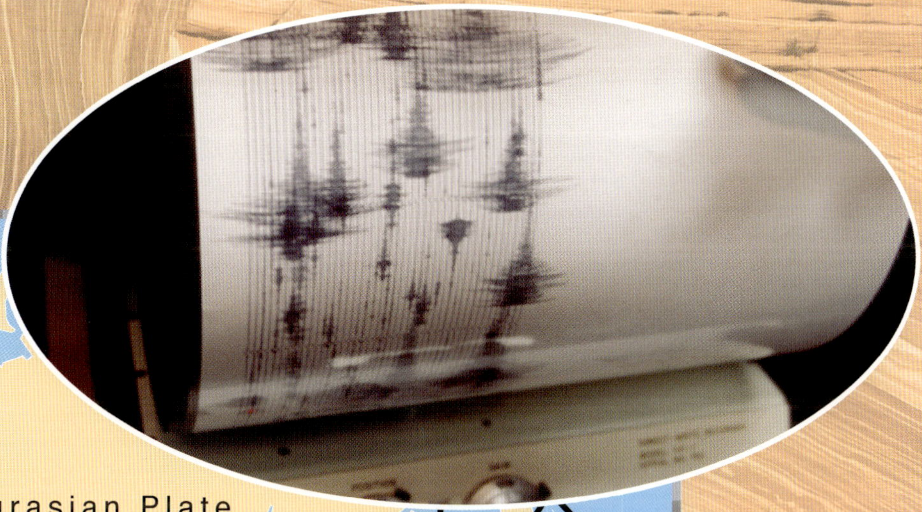

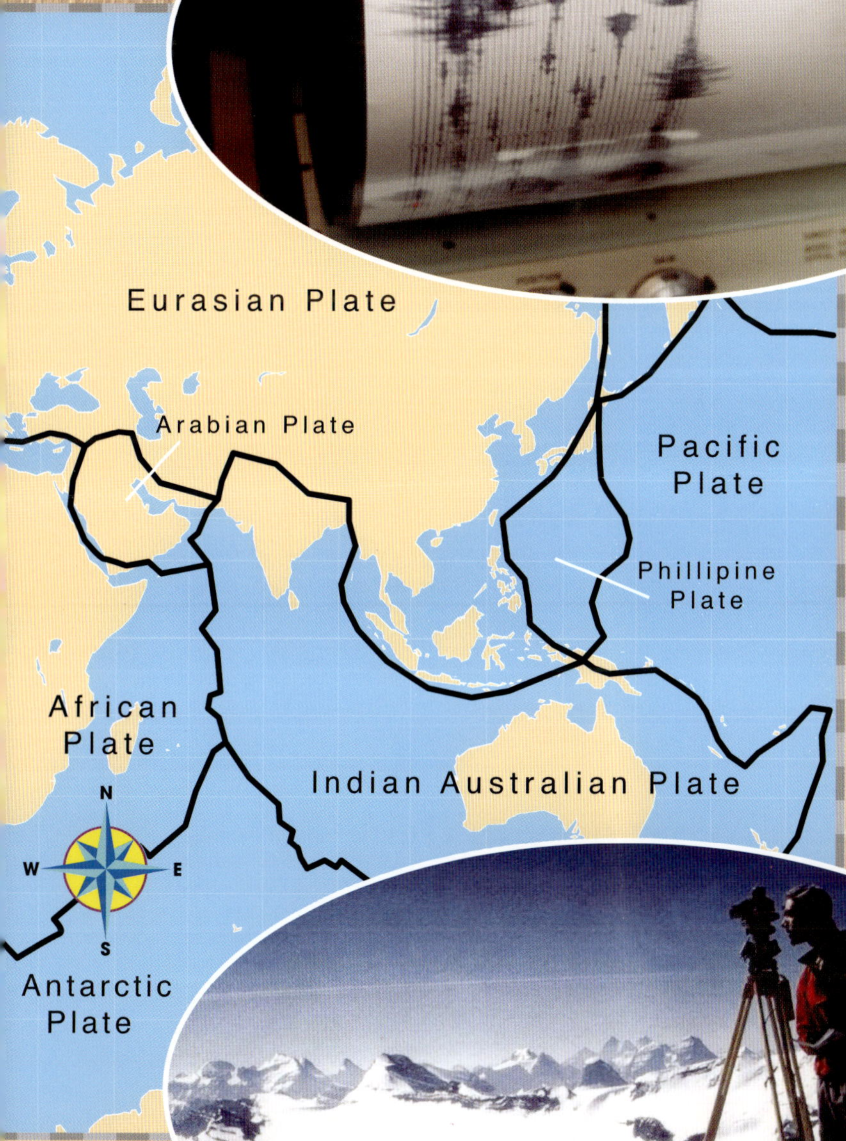
Eurasian Plate
Arabian Plate
Pacific Plate
Phillipine Plate
African Plate
Indian Australian Plate
Antarctic Plate
N
S
E
W

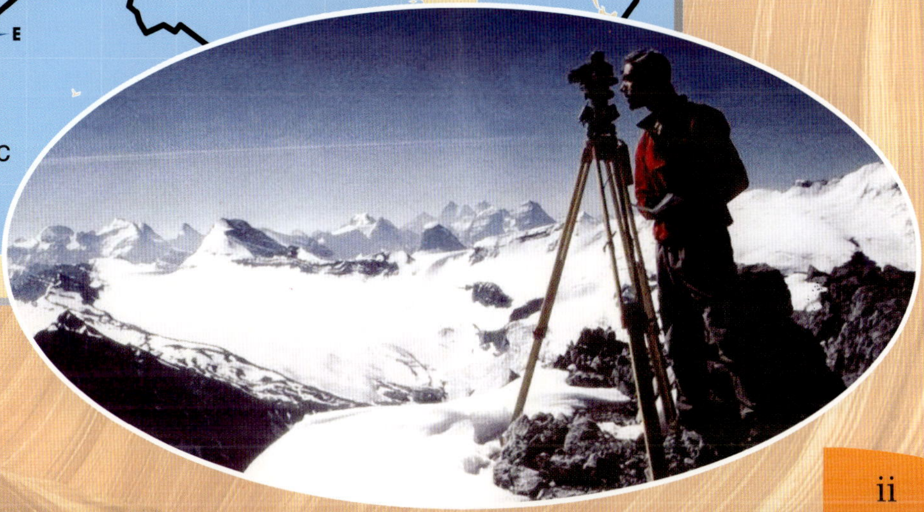

Words To Think About

Characteristics
- made of ice
- slow-moving
- ?

glacier
What do you think the word **glacier** means?

Examples
- Ruth Glacier
- St. Mary's Glacier
- ?

fault
What do you think the word **fault** means in this book?

Meaning 1
a mistake or weakness (noun)

Meaning 2
to make a mistake (verb)

Meaning 3
a crack in Earth's crust (noun)

Read for More Clues

erosion,	page 2
fault,	page 5
glacier,	page 2

erosion

What do you think the word erosion means?

What can cause erosion?
- wind
- ?
- rain

What can erosion do?
- wash away beaches
- ?
- wear away mountains

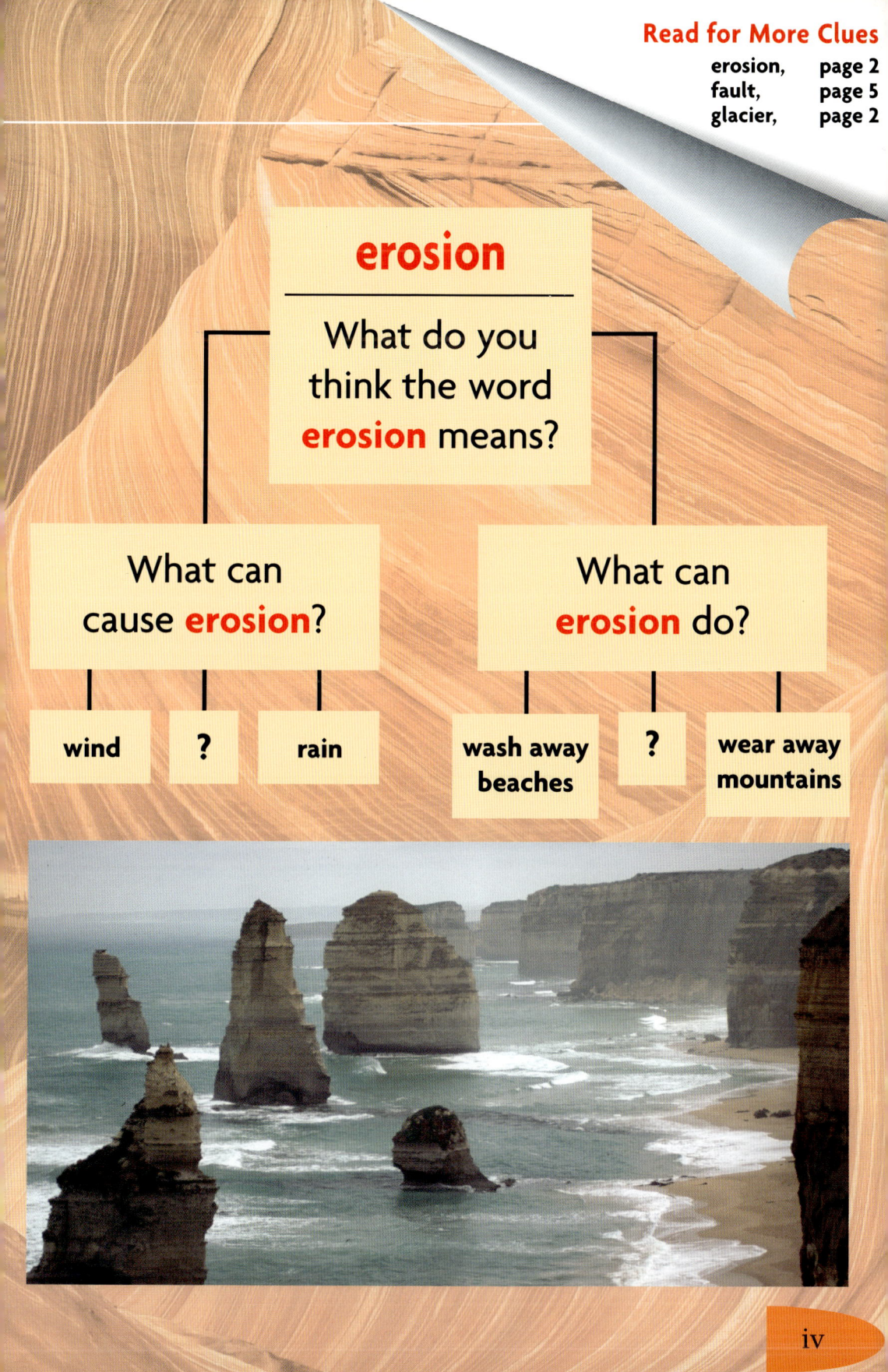

iv

Introduction

Earth is changing all the time. Different **forces** (FORS-uz) cause these changes. What are these forces?

Earthquakes (ERTH-kwakes) are a kind of force. They can change Earth's shape very fast. **Glaciers** (GLAY-sherz) are another force. Glaciers are giant chunks of ice. They move rocks and dirt. Wind and water are forces, too. They can cause **erosion** (ih-ROH-zhun). Erosion is the wearing away of dirt, rocks, and sand.

◀ The Lambert Glacier in Antarctica is over 200 miles (320 kilometers) long. It is one of the largest glaciers in the world.

▲ sand dune in Namibia

Scientists can measure all these forces. Scientists measure how strong earthquakes are. They measure how fast glaciers move. They measure how fast erosion takes place.

Read on to learn more about these forces. Find out how these forces are measured.

CHAPTER 1

Earthquakes

What is an earthquake? First, you have to know about Earth. Earth has three layers. They are the core, the mantle, and the crust. Take a look at the diagram below. The core is in the center of Earth. The mantle wraps around the core. The top part of the mantle is hot, melted rock. The crust floats on top of the mantle.

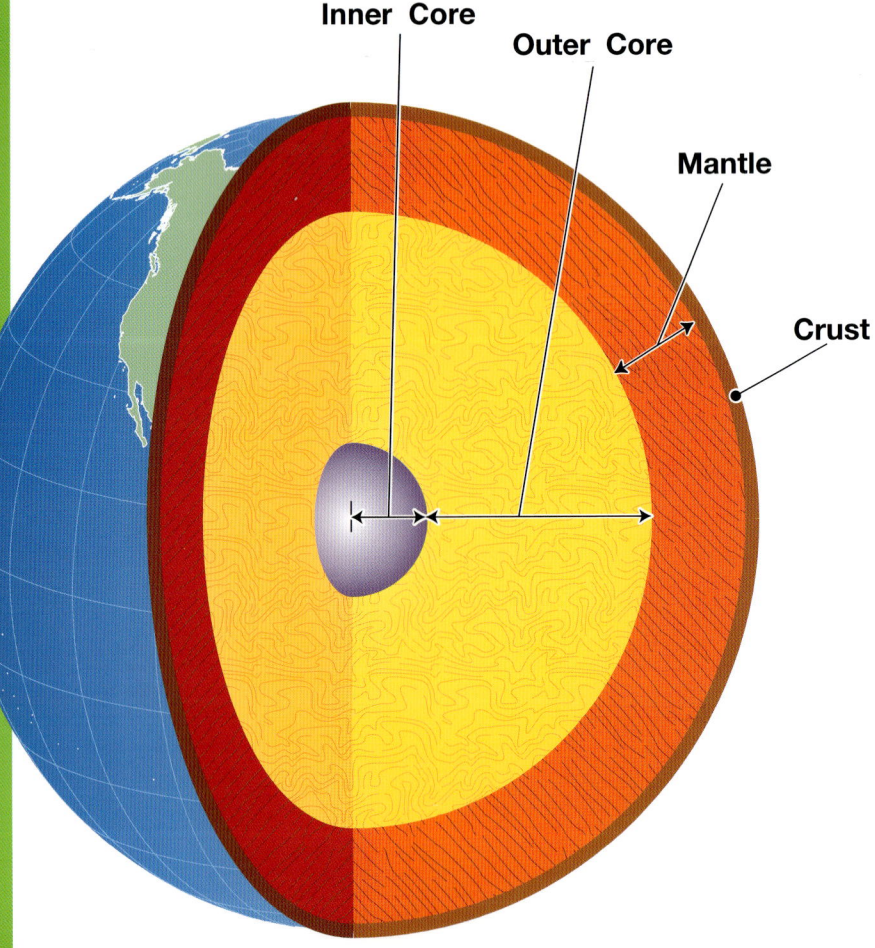

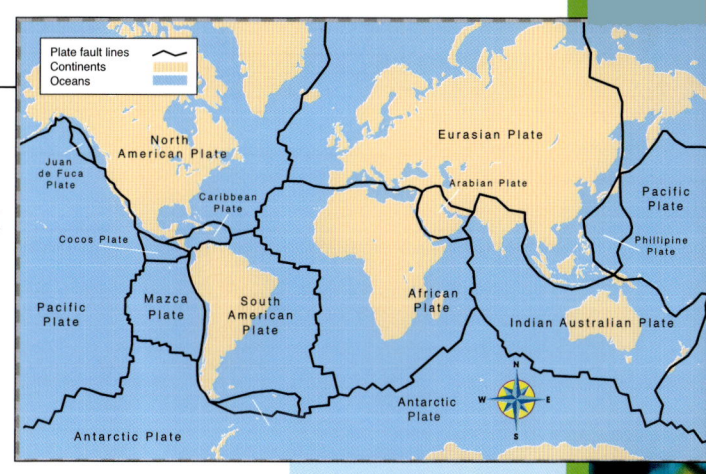

Earth's crust is broken up into giant **plates**. These plates are like huge, flat boats. They float on Earth's mantle. The plates move all the time.

Earth's crust has many cracks in it. These cracks are called **faults**. Sometimes a plate gets stuck along a fault. The plate pushes hard to get free. Suddenly it moves. The force of its move shakes everything in its path. Earth's crust starts to shake. That is an earthquake.

▲ Earthquakes take place at the edges of Earth's plates.

▲ Many earthquakes occur along the San Andreas Fault.

It's a Fact

There are about 1,000 earthquakes around the world every day. Most of them are too small to feel. Only about 150 earthquakes per year are strong enough to feel.

CHAPTER 1

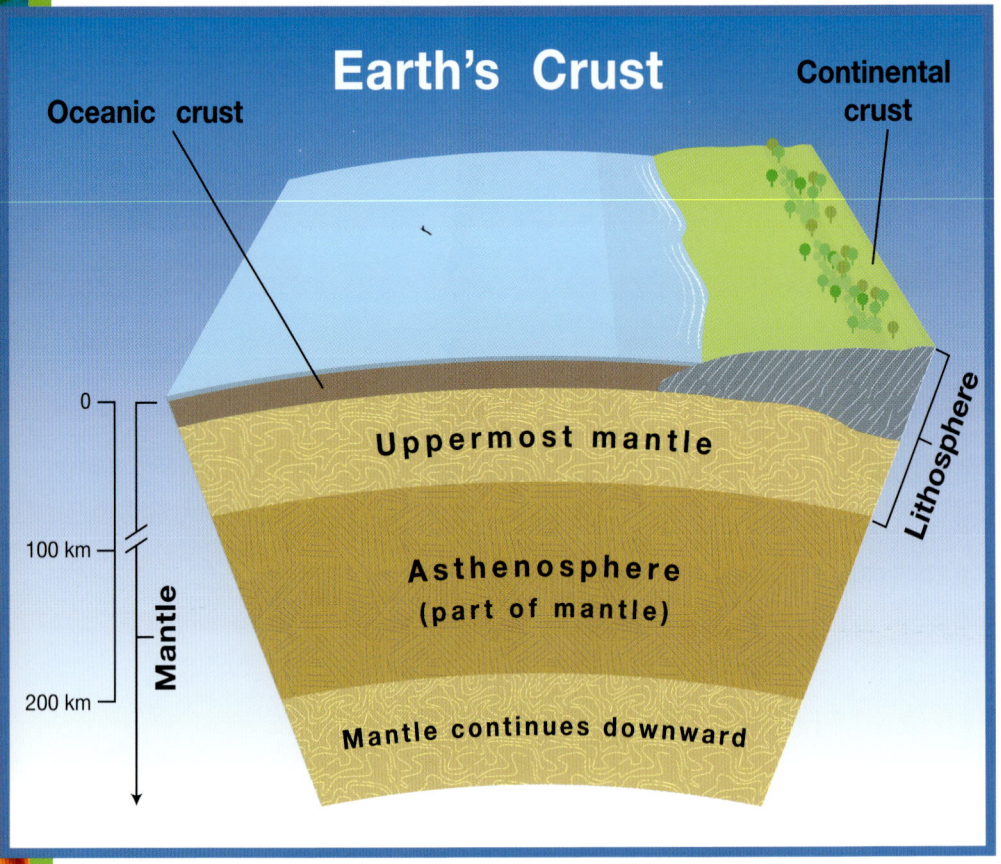

The strongest force of the earthquake is felt at the **epicenter** (EH-pih-sen-ter). That is the point on Earth's crust just above where the earthquake starts.

EARTHQUAKES

How Are Earthquakes Measured?

Special scientists called **seismologists** (size-MAH-luh-jists) measure how strong earthquakes are. They use a machine called a **seismograph** (SIZE-muh-graf). It picks up the movements of Earth's plates. It shows the movements as wavy lines.

▼ These machines are seismographs. The word part *seismo* means "about earthquakes." The word part *graph* means "write."

CHAPTER 1

1. Solve This

Here are three seismograms (SIZE-muh-grams) from an earthquake that happened in Alaska on October 23, 2002. The earthquake was recorded on seismographs around the world.

How much longer did it take for the shock waves to reach Australia than to reach Massachusetts?

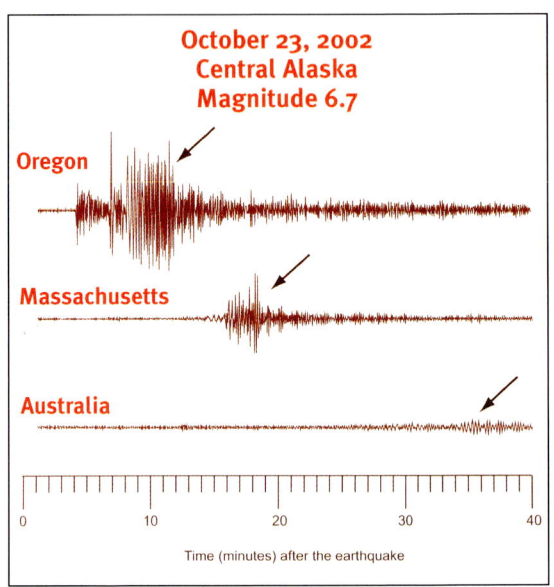

What information from the seismograms do you need to solve the problem?

EARTHQUAKES

The Richter Scale

Scientists compare how strong earthquakes are. Scientists use a special scale, or measuring tool, for this. It is called the Richter (RIK-ter) scale.

The Richter scale has numbers from 1 to 10. The numbers show the strength of the earthquake. The smallest earthquake measures 0 on the Richter scale.

Each number on the scale is ten times stronger than the number just below it. A 2 is ten times stronger than a 1. Earthquakes that measure less than 3 are barely felt. Earthquakes above 5 change Earth's crust.

2. Solve This

The strength of an earthquake is called its **magnitude**. A magnitude 5 earthquake is how many times stronger than a magnitude 3 earthquake?

MATH ✓ POINT

What information from the text do you need to answer the question?

THEY MADE A DIFFERENCE

Dr. Charles Richter developed the Richter scale in 1935. The Richter scale has been used to measure earthquakes on the moon and Mars!

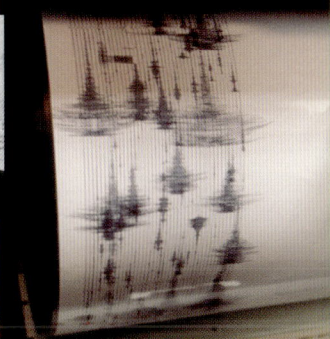

a seismograph reading ▶

9

CHAPTER 1

Scientists study the movement of Earth's plates. This helps them watch for earthquakes.

Careers in Science

Geology is the study of Earth, its rocks and landforms, and its changes. Some geologists study earthquakes. They might walk through the mountains for three or four weeks. They use seismographs to find places where earthquakes might happen.

▲ Geologist Dr. Avouac reads recordings from a seismograph.

EARTHQUAKES

▲ Laser beams can measure tiny movements along a fault.

CHAPTER 1

A Terrible Earthquake

On December 26, 2004, a huge earthquake shook South Asia. Its epicenter was deep in the Indian Ocean. The earthquake caused **tsunamis** (soo-NAH-meez). These are giant waves.

The giant waves hit many countries on the Indian Ocean. The waves covered small islands. They moved tons of sand and soil. The waves changed the land. They did this in a few hours.

 POINT

Read More About It
Read more about the tsunami at your school library or local library. Find out how people around the world have helped tsunami victims.

◀ Look at the way the tsunami changed this coastline in India.

12

CHAPTER 2

Glaciers

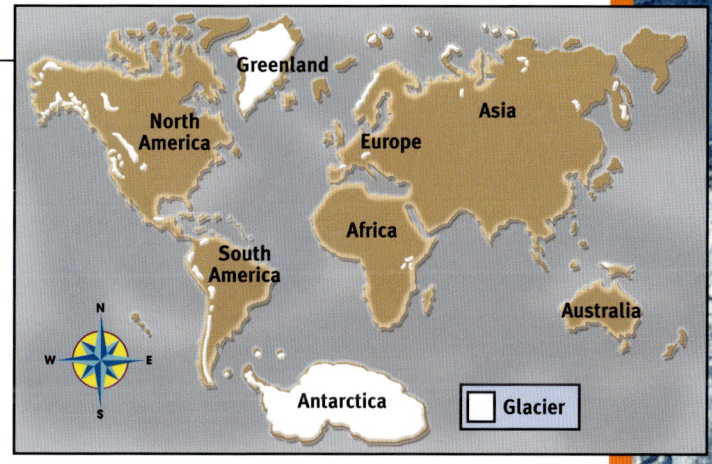

Glaciers cover an area of Earth about the size of Canada! Huge glaciers called ice sheets cover all of Antarctica (ant-ARK-tih-kuh). They cover most of Greenland, too. Take a look at the map above.

These giant chunks of ice can be different sizes. Some are as big as a football field. Others are as much as 60 miles (100 kilometers) long.

It's a Fact

The ice sheet on Antarctica is more than 2 miles (3 kilometers) thick.

CHAPTER 2

3. Solve This

One meter is equal to about 3 feet. Suppose a glacier is 60 meters thick. About how thick is the glacier in feet?

MATH ✔ POINT

Is your answer an estimate of how thick the glacier is? Or does your answer tell exactly how thick the glacier is? How do you know?

How Do Glaciers Form?

Glaciers form in cold places. They form in high mountains and at the North and South Poles. Snow falls each year. The summers are cool, so all the snow doesn't melt. Each winter, new snow falls on the old snow. The weight of the new snow packs the old snow down.

In time, the old snow changes to solid ice. The ice gets thicker and thicker. These changes go on for thousands of years.

▲ A glacier becomes heavier and heavier as the ice builds up in layers. The great weight causes a glacier to move.

14

GLACIERS

▲ Glaciers on Alaska's College Fjord

How Do Glaciers Move?

Glaciers are very heavy. Their great weight makes them move. They move very slowly. The average speed of a glacier is less than 2 feet (.6 meter) per year.

Sometimes there is water under a glacier. The water can cause the glacier to slide down a mountain.

4. Solve This

Glaciers move at different rates. Suppose one glacier moved down a mountain at 98 feet (30 meters) per year.
a. How much would the glacier move in two years?
b. How much would the glacier move in six months?

MATH  POINT

What strategies did you use to answers these questions?

15

CHAPTER 2

How Are Glaciers Measured?

Scientists measure how much glaciers grow and melt. They can learn about changes in Earth's climate this way. They can also watch out for floods or other problems. Here are some ways to measure glaciers.

1.

▲ Scientists can use a laser in a small airplane to measure the height of glaciers.

16

GLACIERS

2.

◀ A scientist uses lasers to measure the height of glaciers in the Canadian Rockies. In two years, he will measure these glaciers again. This way, he can tell how much they have changed.

3.

▲ From space, special cameras on satellites (SA-tuh-lites) take pictures and measure glaciers. Scientists compare the measurements and photos. They can see how glaciers are changing.

5. Solve This

Suppose a glacier melted 12 inches (30 centimeters) in one year. If it melted at about the same rate each year, how much would the glacier melt in 50 years? Give your answer in inches and in centimeters.

MATH ✓ POINT

Is your answer the exact amount the glacier would melt in 50 years, or is it an estimate? How do you know?

17

CHAPTER 2

How Far and How Fast?

Scientists also measure how far and how fast glaciers move. They put rows of sticks into the glacier ice. These sticks move as the glacier moves.

After a few months, the scientists look at where the sticks are. This tells them how far and how fast the glacier has moved. They can keep checking over a period of time. This gives them a history of how the glacier moves.

6. Solve This

Glaciers that move quickly are called galloping (GA-lup-ing) glaciers. The fastest galloping glacier moved 26,896 feet (8,200 meters) in 82 days. The glacier moved at the same rate every day.
a. How many feet did the glacier move in one day?
b. How many meters did the glacier move in one day?

◀ The fastest galloping glacier is in the Himalaya (hih-muh-LAY-uh) Mountains.

MATH ✓ POINT

How could you check your answers?

18

GLACIERS

▲ The Matterhorn (MA-ter-horn) is a mountain in Switzerland. Glaciers carved its strange shape.

Glaciers Cause Erosion

Glaciers change the land they cross through erosion. Glaciers are hard and very heavy. They can scrape the mountains. They make deep scratches in rocks. They loosen bits of dirt and rock called **debris** (duh-BREE). The dirt and rock are carried along with the ice. Glaciers can cut into mountains. Glaciers can change their shape.

Glaciers can also dig deep holes in the soft rock they rest on. The glaciers melt. Then the holes fill with water and become lakes.

CHAPTER 2

▲ It took thousands of years for glaciers to carve the bed of this lake.

The Ice Age

Some glaciers have been around for about one million years. About 20,000 years ago, huge glaciers moved and covered parts of North America, Europe, and Asia. This time is known as the last Ice Age.

About 6,000 years ago, the Ice Age glaciers started to melt. They left giant rocks and other debris behind. You can still find some of these rocks and debris today.

20

GLACIERS

Glacial (GLAY-shul) erosion smoothed these large rocks. ▶

Glaciers carved canyons in the Rocky Mountains. ▶

Glaciers took along loose rock as they moved. When the glaciers melted, they left piles of this loose rock behind. ▶

THEY MADE A DIFFERENCE

Jean Louis Agassiz (A-guh-see) studied glaciers near his home in Switzerland. He saw that the glaciers left scratches in rocks and piles of debris. Then he saw those marks in places that did not have glaciers. Agassiz thought great glaciers had once covered the land during an ice age. Other scientists studied his work, and decided that he was right.

CHAPTER 3

Water and Wind Erosion

▲ These rocks off the coast of Australia used to be part of the rocky cliffs.

Waves and wind cause erosion on the beach. Waves and wind move the sand around. Storms drag lots of sand into the water. This kind of erosion can be very fast. One big storm can wash away a beach!

Waves and wind wear away rocks near the beach, too. Over time, erosion turns the rocks into caves, arches, and other shapes. This kind of erosion takes a long time.

22

Rivers and Rain

Rivers move all the time. They pick up dirt and rocks. The moving water carries the dirt and rocks along with it. Over time, rivers can carve deep canyons through rock.

Rain beats down on rocks. It can wear them down. Rain can carry away bits of sand and dirt. Floods can cause erosion very fast.

7. Solve This

The Cape Hatteras (HA-tuh-rus) lighthouse in North Carolina was built in 1870. It was 1,500 feet (457 meters) from the ocean's edge. By 1999, the lighthouse stood only 150 feet (45 meters) from the ocean.
a. How much beach eroded between 1870 and 1999?
b. How many years did that erosion take?
c. Was the lighthouse farther away from the ocean after it was moved in 1999? Or was it farther away from the ocean in 1870? By how much?

MATH ✔ POINT

What information do you need to answer question c? Where can you find this information?

▲ This lighthouse was moved one-half mile from the ocean in 1999.

CHAPTER 3

Wind Erosion

Wind can change Earth in two ways. A strong wind can lift small bits of dust, dirt, and sand into the air. These bits might travel many miles. Then they drop to the ground. Over time, wind can take away all of the dirt from a place. Only rock is left.

Wind also pushes dirt and sand against rocks. The dirt and sand rub against the rock. Some of the rock wears away.

▲ Wind erosion helped shape this toadstool rock.

WATER AND WIND EROSION

Wind can harm land where there are no plants. In many parts of the world, farmers have cleared land to grow crops. They have cut down all the trees. Trees and plants keep soil in place. Without them, the wind can blow away rich soil. Farmers try to stop erosion. They plant trees and bushes to stop the wind.

It's a Fact

In parts of Australia, sheep, cattle, and rabbits have eaten away plants in open areas. The wind carries away the earth. A huge dust storm in Melbourne in 1983 moved about two million tons of dust and dirt.

▲ Windbreaks on these fields slow down the speed of the wind.

CHAPTER 3

Measuring Erosion

Scientists use pins to measure soil erosion. They stick the pins in the ground. They leave the top of the pin sticking out. They mark the part of the pin that touches the ground.

The scientists come back later. They know the soil has eroded if the mark on the pin is higher.

Everyday Science

Earthworms help keep soil from eroding. The worms dig holes in the ground. During rain, the water flows into the ground. It does not erode the earth on top.

26

WATER AND WIND EROSION

▲ eroded sandstone in Arizona

There is another way to measure soil erosion. People paint a line around a rock. They paint it just above where the rock meets the ground. The eroding soil leaves an unpainted strip below the line. People measure the unpainted strip to find out how much the soil has eroded.

CHAPTER 3

Humans Cause Erosion, Too

People cut down trees and bushes. They clear land to farm or to build. The roots of trees and plants hold soil in place. Without them, dry soil or mud can slide down a hill. Landslides and mudslides can kill people and destroy homes.

▲ Haiti

In Haiti, people cut down the forests to build houses. The bare soil eroded. Heavy rains come often in Haiti. Landslides destroyed many homes there.

THEY MADE A DIFFERENCE

George Washington Carver studied plants and farming. Carver showed farmers how to plant crops that made the earth better. He told farmers to change their crops around, too. They stopped planting the same crop in the same place all the time. Carver's methods helped stop erosion.

✓ POINT   Make Connections

Talk with people in your neighborhood who have gardens. Ask them how they prevent erosion. What could you do to prevent or lessen the effects of erosion?

Conclusion

You have seen that Earth changes all the time. Some of the forces that cause those changes are earthquakes, glaciers, water, and wind. Some of these forces are fast and some are slow.

Scientists are working to find good ways to measure these forces. They want to learn as much as they can about them. That way, they can help us protect ourselves from the dangers they bring. They can also teach us how to protect Earth.

Solve This

Answers

1. Page 8
17 minutes. Subtract 18 from 35.
Math Checkpoint
You need to know the time when the earthquake hit Australia and the time when it hit Massachusetts.

2. Page 9
100 times
Math Checkpoint
"Each number on the scale is ten times stronger than the number just below it."

3. Page 14
about 180 feet
60 meters x 3 feet = 180 feet.
Math Checkpoint
It is an estimate. The problem says one meter is equal to about 3 feet. The question asks about how thick the glacier is in feet.

4. Page 15
a. 196 feet.
98 feet x 2 years = 196 feet.
b. 49 feet. Divide 98 feet by two, because six months is half a year. 98 feet divided by 2 = 49 feet.
Math Checkpoint
a. multiplication
b. division

5. Page 17
600 inches. 12 inches a year x 50 years = 600 inches
1,500 centimeters. 30 centimeters a year x 50 years = 1,500 centimeters.
Math Checkpoint
It is an estimate. The problem says the glacier melts at about the same rate each year.

6. Page 18
a. 328 feet per day. 26,896 feet divided by 82 days = 328 feet per day.
b. 100 meters per day. 8,200 meters by 82 days = 100 meters per day.
Math Checkpoint
a. multiply 328 feet per day x 82 days = 26,896 feet
b. multiply 100 meters per day x 82 days = 8,200 meters

7. Page 23
a. 1,350 feet. 1,500 feet − 150 feet = 1,350 feet.
412 meters. 457 meters − 45 meters = 412 meters.
b. 129 years. 1999 − 1870 = 129 years.
c. The lighthouse was 1,140 feet farther from the ocean after it was moved in 1999. In 1870 it was 1,500 feet from the ocean. In 1999 it was moved one-half mile (2,640 feet) from the ocean. 2,640 feet − 1,500 feet = 1,140 feet.
Math Checkpoint
The photo caption says the lighthouse was moved one-half mile away from the ocean in 1999.

Glossary

debris (duh-BREE) bits of rock and soil that are loosened by glaciers (page 19)

earthquake (ERTH-kwake) a shaking or trembling of Earth's crust (page 2)

epicenter (EH-pih-sen-ter) the place on the surface of the Earth just above where an earthquake starts (page 6)

erosion (ih-ROH-zhun) process that moves rocks, dirt, and sand from one place to another (page 2)

fault (FALLT) the boundary between two tectonic plates; a crack in the earth caused by movement of the plates (page 5)

force (FORS) a pushing or pulling action (page 2)

glacier (GLAY-sher) a huge mass of ice and snow that moves under its own weight (page 2)

magnitude (MAG-nuh-tood) the strength or power of an earthquake (page 9)

plate (PLATE) a section of the Earth's crust (page 5)

seismograph (SIZE-muh-graf) a machine that measures waves from an earthquake (page 7)

seismologist (size-MAH-luh-jist) a scientist who studies earthquakes (page 7)

tsunami (soo-NAH-mee) a huge wave often created by an earthquake (page 12)

Index

Agassiz, Jean Louis, 21
Antarctica, 2, 13
Carver, George Washington, 28
core, 4
crust, 4–6, 9
debris, 19–21
earthquake, 2–10, 12, 29
epicenter, 6, 12
erosion, 2–3, 21–28
fault, 5, 11
force, 2–3, 5–6, 29
geology, 10
glacier, 2–3, 13–21, 29
Haiti, 28
Ice Age, 20–21

ice sheet, 13
laser beams, 11, 16–17
magnitude, 9
mantle, 4–5
plate, 5, 7, 10
rain, 23, 26, 28
Richter, Charles, 9
Richter scale, 9
rivers, 23
seismograph, 7–10
seismologist, 7
tsunami, 12
water, 2, 15, 19, 22–23, 26, 29
wind, 2, 22, 24–25, 29